THE
CONTENT
DEFICIT

Bridging the Gap for Modern Business Owners

By

Dallen Taylor

Table of Contents

Acknowledgments

F

irst and foremost, I want to express my deepest gratitude to **Tavarus Dove**. Your trust in Simply Edit Pro and your unwavering commitment to excellence made this journey not only possible but truly inspiring. Working alongside you and your incredible team has been a privilege. Your passion and drive have pushed the boundaries of what we can achieve together, and for that, I am profoundly thankful.

I would also like to extend a heartfelt thank you to **Daniel Priestley**. Your wisdom and insights have been instrumental in shaping my approach to business and content strategy. Your work has been a guiding light throughout this project, and your influence is woven into the very fabric of this book.

To everyone who has contributed to this endeavor, whether through support, collaboration, or inspiration, I am deeply grateful. This book is a testament to the power of teamwork, shared vision, and the relentless pursuit of excellence.

Thank you.

CHAPTER 1

The Content Deficit Crisis

I

n today's fast-paced digital landscape, there's a growing crisis that many business owners are unaware of—a content deficit. This isn't just a minor gap; it's a chasm that can determine whether a business thrives or fades into obscurity. The reality is stark: **over68% of businesses report that they can only produce half the content needed to stay visible in a crowded marketplace.** That means more than half of the businesses operating today are struggling to meet even the basic content requirements to remain competitive.

So, what exactly are those minimum requirements? To maintain visibility in the current digital arena, businesses must produce at least 16 posts per month across four different platforms. This is the bare minimum to simply cut through the noise. But if you've ever tried to keep up with this demand, you know it's easier said than done. Consistently developing and producing content month after month is a daunting task, especially without a strategic approach. Without a solid plan, businesses risk falling behind, losing relevance, and ultimately, failing in today's market.

But just how significant is this deficit? Consider this: businesses that exceed the minimum requirement of 16 posts per month see **3.5 times more traffic than those that post only once a week or fewer.** This isn't just a difference in engagement—it's a difference in potential revenue. Imagine how much money your business could be leaving on the table by not consistently meeting or exceeding these content benchmarks. For larger businesses, the stakes are even higher; the bigger the business, the greater the potential loss.

So, what's the solution? How can businesses not only meet but surpass these content requirements to ensure they stand out and succeed in a saturated market? This book will explore the strategies and systems necessary to overcome the content deficit, enabling you to not just survive, but thrive in today's competitive landscape.

CHAPTER 2

My Story - The Founder's Journey

Dallen Taylor's Story and the Founding of Simply Edit Pro

A

t 22 years old, I found myself standing at a crossroads that would define the rest of my life. I had secured a full-ride scholarship to a university out of state, eager to dive into a business program that I believed would equip me with the tools to take my production company to new heights. But it didn't take long for reality to set in. Within a few months of starting classes, I realized that the traditional education system was not going to work for me.

I was excited about the promise of a business degree, but the curriculum quickly became a source of frustration. While I found value in the finance and accounting courses, the marketing and public relations classes felt outdated—disconnected from the fast-paced digital world where I was already running my business. It wasn't just the content that bothered me; it was the disconnect between academia and real-world experience. When I discovered that none of my professors had ever owned or operated a business, it hit me hard. How could they teach me to build something they had never done themselves?

The frustration built up until I couldn't ignore it any longer. I knew I needed to make a change. Dropping out of college was one of the hardest decisions I've ever made. The anxiety was overwhelming—not just because of the uncertainty of my future, but because of the disappointment I knew I'd see in my family's eyes. I went as far as faking transcripts and class assignments to keep up appearances, but deep down, I knew this charade couldn't last. After three agonizing months, I finally told my family the truth. The disappointment on their faces was palpable—it was the most I'd ever seen. They were from a different time, a time when a degree was the golden ticket to success. But I knew that in the rapidly evolving digital age, I had to forge my own path.

That disappointment, however, became my fuel. I realized that if I wanted my dream job, I'd have to build it myself. From a young age, I had worked nearly 15 different jobs— —from construction to waiting tables—and I understood the value of hard work. But more importantly, I learned that the only way to truly have the job you want is to create it. And so, I founded Simply Edit Pro.

The mission was clear: combine my expertise in software and traditional video production to create a service that would provide clients with more leads and top-notch recruitment strategies. I wish I could say that after dropping out, I hit the ground running, but the reality was different. I moved back home to Seattle, WA, and took a 9-to-5 job. In every spare moment, I was researching, experimenting, and trying to figure out who my target audience was and which industry I should focus on.

My break came when I was hired as the Chief Marketing Officer for a local real estate team. This position became a launchpad, giving me the opportunity to test and develop services that I could later package and market to other industries. It was here that Simply Edit Pro truly began to take shape.

So, let me introduce myself properly: My name is Dallen Taylor, and I'm the founder of Simply Edit Pro—a modern AI marketing agency hyper-focused on making content creation easier and smarter for businesses everywhere. My team of brilliant individuals helps me execute the campaigns that you'll learn about today, and I'm excited to share them with you.

But what does it really mean to be hyper-focused on making content creation easier and smarter? Simply Edit Pro was born out of recognizing a growing gap—the content deficit—between what businesses need to stay competitive and the time and resources they have available. The numbers don't lie: businesses that fail to meet their content demands are leaving significant opportunities on the table.

Let's talk about how companies like Simply Edit Pro bridge that gap. It all begins with a focused approach, starting with redefining your vision. Many of you have a good understanding of your brand and goals, but often, the power of clarity is underestimated. It's the one decision that makes a thousand others possible.

CHAPTER 3

Defining Your Brand

The Power of Brand Identity

W

hen clients first approach my team, they often have the basics—
like a logo and a website—already in place. But these are just the
surface-level elements of a brand. What they often lack is a deep
understanding of their true strengths, their audience, and the
goals they need to achieve to connect with consumers in a
meaningful way.

At Simply Edit Pro, we break down these overarching objectives
into three simple yet powerful pillars: Define, Develop, and
Launch. These pillars are the foundation of a successful brand
strategy, and they guide everything we do.

- **Define:** In this phase, we focus on defining the
  brand's identity, understanding the target audience,
  and identifying the key topics that will resonate
  with your consumers. This clarity is crucial because
  it sets the stage for everything that follows.

- **Develop:** Here, we delve into developing products,
  crafting effective distribution strategies, and
  leveraging cutting-edge AI tools combined with
  new-age processes to move faster and smarter than
  ever before. For instance, we've mastered the art of
  creating a year's worth of content in just a matter of

8

days—transforming what seems like an impossible task into a streamlined process.

- **Launch:** Finally, we'll show you how to effectively launch those products, utilizing content structures that are systemized, manageable, and scalable. This is where your vision becomes reality, and we'll ensure that your launch strategy is as powerful as the brand you've built.

Starting with a well-defined brand is incredibly powerful, and I'm going to show you why. We'll then move on to product development, distribution strategies, and the actual production process tailored for business owners who don't have the time to create these systems themselves. Lastly, we'll dive into some of the powerful AI-driven techniques that Simply Edit Pro is pioneering, and show you how to launch, systemize, manage, and grow your brand effectively.

Brand Identity in Action: The Dove Mastery Project

Every brand has a unique identity, and it's crucial to define both its strengths and goals right from the start. Let's take a look at a real-world example: the Dove Mastery Project, a campaign Simply Edit Pro developed for Tavarus Dove, an established speaker, coach, and financial expert.

The key insight here is that people fall in love with people, not faceless brands. A brand's success often hinges on having a high-value ambassador—a key person of influence who embodies the brand's values and connects with the audience on a personal level. This concept is supported by the social theory known as Dunbar's Number, proposed by Professor Robin Dunbar. According to Dunbar, to earn a place in someone's trust circle, you need to spend a minimum of 7 hours across 11 interactions in 4 different locations. This is a significant challenge, especially when considering that 68% of business owners are already struggling to meet the minimum content requirements.

Let's break this down with an example. Imagine walking down a busy street and suddenly spotting a dear friend 20 feet ahead. Your brain lights up with recognition. But if I asked you to describe the last three people you walked by to get to that friend, you'd likely struggle. This is your brain's limbic system at work, filtering out people who haven't spent enough time getting to know you. It's the same mechanism that helps consumers filter out brands they haven't built a connection with.

Consider this: if you've ever been in the market for a specific car, you've probably noticed that once you start looking, you see that car everywhere. This is the power of breaking through a consumer's "cloaking device" by consistently showing up. Google conducted a study showing that it takes over 11 touchpoints for the average consumer to consider making a purchase. This aligns perfectly with Dunbar's findings—7 hours, 11 interactions, 4 locations—to build trust and familiarity.

So, how do you implement these concepts into your business? Start by asking, "Who is the key person of influence in my business?" This phrase, coined by Daniel Priestley, is essential to understanding who will become the face of your brand—the person your consumers will come to know, like, and trust over time.

Applying Clarity to Your Brand

No matter where you are in your business journey, you can always gain more clarity to improve. When defining your brand, start by creating an updated list of your business's strengths and goals. Let's revisit the Dove Mastery Project to illustrate these concepts in context.

Tavarus Dove had clear strengths and goals: he wanted to develop monetized products that leveraged his expertise and ultimately served his audience. We translated these goals into a set of actionable objectives:

- The conception and development of a new brand.

- A comprehensive website to host coaching programs, book speaking engagements, and offer financial services.

- A course on mastering sales, communication, and personal finance.

- A book that captures Tavarus's key concepts and pivotal moments.

Through collaboration, we were able to build a brand identity that not only reflected Tavarus's strengths but also resonated deeply with his target audience. This is the power of defining your brand with clarity and purpose—creating a roadmap that guides every decision, every piece of content, and every interaction with your audience.

Defining the Foundation: The Dove Mastery Brand

As we've discussed, the process we use at Simply Edit Pro revolves around three key pillars: Define, Develop, and Launch. Each step is crucial in building a strong, cohesive— —brand that can stand the test of time. Let's dive into the first pillar: Define.

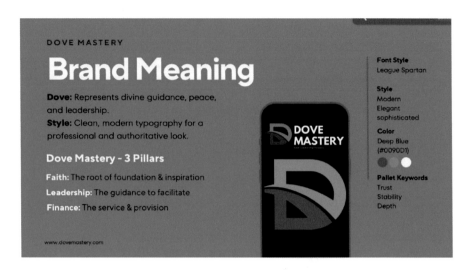

When we partnered with Tavarus Dove, our goal was to create a brand that truly reflected his values, strengths, and aspirations. The brand we developed was called Dove Mastery. The design of the logo was intentional and symbolic—the "D" represents a swoosh that resembles a road. This road is not just a path; it's the road to faith, leadership, and financial empowerment. Every element of the brand was thoughtfully crafted to ensure that it resonated with Tavarus's vision and connected with his audience on a deeper level.

The importance of establishing a well-thought-out brand from the very beginning cannot be overstated. When done right, defining your brand becomes the catalyst for a snowball effect, making it easier to template and scale your business as it grows. Unfortunately, many business owners miss out on this critical step, often jumping straight into development without a clear definition of their brand identity. This lack of clarity can lead to fragmented efforts and missed opportunities.

One of the key components of the Dove Mastery brand was the creation of an in-house academy to host all of Tavarus's branded products. We named it the Leaders— —Academy, which added depth and organization to the overall brand.

This academy serves as a central hub where clients can engage with Tavarus's offerings in a structured and cohesive way.

Putting Definition into Practice

Defining the two core sectors of Dove Mastery's offerings may seem like a straightforward task, but it's a foundational step that creates clarity and enhances the user experience for potential clients. Here's how we approached it:

Sector 1: Services

The first sector covers the services offered on the Dove Mastery website. This includes group coaching, one-on-one coaching, and speaking engagements, all of which can be booked directly through the site. By clearly defining these services, we made it easier for clients to understand what Tavarus offers and how they can benefit from his expertise.

Sector 2: Products

The second sector, represented as a distinct tab on the website, focuses on products such as courses, books, and workshops. Clients can easily purchase these offerings through the site, creating a seamless and organized experience.

By segmenting the services and products into these two sectors, we enhanced the readability and usability of the website for new potential clients.

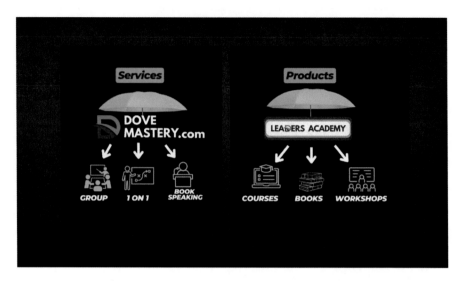

What's remarkable about this approach is that we were able to define and organize Tavarus's strengths and goals into a coherent structure before any website or tangible product was even created. This demonstrates the power of the Define phase—it lays the groundwork for everything that follows, ensuring that each subsequent step is aligned with the brand's core identity.

By taking the time to define your brand with clarity and purpose, you're not just setting up a business; you're building a strong foundation that will support and guide all your future efforts. The process of defining your brand might seem abstract at first, but as you can see from the Dove Mastery example, it's a crucial step that can significantly impact the success of your business.

CHAPTER 4

Audience and Topics

The Importance of Defining Your Audience

O

ne of the most powerful outcomes of a well-defined brand is the ability to create a comprehensive profile of your target audience. As we discussed earlier, the defining process generates a compounding snowball effect—once you've established the core elements of your brand, everything else becomes easier to define. This is particularly true when it comes to identifying and understanding your audience.

In the case of Dove Mastery, this process allowed us to quickly and effectively create a detailed audience profile for Tavarus. The clearer your brand identity, the more precise and insightful your audience definition will be. The result is a tailored approach to reaching your ideal customers, ensuring that your content resonates deeply with the people you want to connect with.

The 6 Key Traits of Audience Profiling

At Simply Edit Pro, we utilize six key traits to define our customer demographics. These traits are crucial for creating an accurate and actionable audience profile, and they can be easily applied to any industry:

1. The Who:

This defines the core identity of your audience. In the case of Dove Mastery, the "Who" would be professionals seeking financial and personal growth. Understanding who your audience is at their core is the first step in crafting content that speaks directly to their needs and aspirations.

2. Income:

Understanding the income level of your audience helps you tailor your offerings and marketing messages to match their financial capacity. For Dove Mastery, we focused on high-net-worth individuals who are likely to invest in premium coaching and financial services.

3. Beliefs:

Your audience's beliefs and values are critical in shaping the tone and messaging of your content. For Dove Mastery, the audience leans towards a faith-based perspective, which influenced the topics and themes we emphasized.

4. Goals:

Identifying the goals of your audience allows you to create content that addresses their specific needs and desires. Whether they seek personal growth, financial stability, or spiritual guidance, understanding these goals helps you position your brand as the solution.

5. Age Range:

Knowing the age range of your audience helps you tailor your communication style, content format, and platform choice. Dove Mastery's target audience spans a broad age range, but we particularly focused on those in mid-career stages who are actively seeking growth and improvement.

6. Location:

Location plays a significant role in understanding the cultural context and specific needs of your audience. It also helps in segmenting your market and focusing on areas where your services can have the greatest impact.

Why Audience Definition Matters

Defining your audience is not just a preliminary step; it's a foundational element that drives all other aspects of your marketing strategy. A well-defined audience combined with a strong brand identity will naturally reveal the topics you need to cover to capture your potential clients' attention.

For instance, consider a 2019 study by the Content Marketing Institute, which found that 90% of the most successful content marketers prioritize understanding their audience's informational needs. By knowing who your audience is, what they believe, and what they aspire to achieve, you can create content that not only resonates with them but also builds lasting relationships.

Another compelling statistic from HubSpot's 2020 Marketing Report shows that personalized content tailored to specific audience segments can increase engagement by up to 50%. This demonstrates the power of a well-defined audience profile in crafting content that truly connects.

Applying the 6 Traits: The Dove Mastery Example

Let's take these six traits and see how they were applied in the development of Dove Mastery. By defining the "Who" as professionals seeking financial and personal growth, we were able to craft content that directly addressed the challenges and aspirations of this audience. The focus on high-net-worth individuals ensured that our messaging aligned with the financial expectations and investment capacities of our target market.

The faith-based beliefs of the audience informed the tone and topics of our content, making sure that we addressed their spiritual needs in addition to their financial ones. By understanding their goals—such as gaining financial security, improving personal development, and deepening their spiritual practices—we were able to create a content strategy that was not only relevant but also deeply meaningful.

From Definition to Content Strategy

A well-defined audience profile leads directly to the creation of targeted, impactful content. The topics you choose to cover should stem from the intersection of your audience's goals and your brand's strengths. For Dove Mastery, this meant focusing on topics like faith and spirituality, financial literacy, and personal growth, all viewed through the lens of the six key traits we identified.

By packaging this information into a comprehensive brand development kit, we were able to hand it off to our development team with confidence. This kit included everything from audience demographics to content themes, ensuring that every piece of content produced was aligned with the brand's identity and audience's needs.

Conclusion: The Power of Clarity

In conclusion, the more you define in the beginning, the easier it becomes to define everything else. The process of audience definition not only clarifies who you are speaking to but also what you should be saying. It is the blueprint that guides the development of content, ensuring that every message is on point, relevant, and impactful.

In today's crowded market, where content is abundant but attention is scarce, defining your audience with precision is more critical than ever. It's not just about reaching more people; it's about reaching the right people with the right message at the right time. By doing so, you position your brand as a trusted partner in your audience's journey, leading to deeper engagement, stronger relationships, and ultimately, greater success.

CHAPTER 5

Developing Products

Introduction to Product Development

O

nce you've gained clarity on the necessary products to develop, discovered during the defining process, the next step is to create the myriad of branded assets required for each product. In Tavarus Dove's case, he needed digital assets for his website, course, and book. Many people underestimate the sheer amount of assets needed to bring products like these to life. For the course alone, we had to develop banners, PDFs, digital downloads, custom price tags, quizzes, and more. The website and book also demanded their own unique, custom-branded assets. This can be a daunting task for any production team, let alone a business owner with limited time.

The Six Levels of Branded Assets

To streamline this process, we categorize branded assets into six levels, each aligning with different stages of a customer or product lifecycle. Understanding these levels helps ensure that your brand remains consistent and impactful at every touchpoint.

1. Foundational Brand Identity Assets

These assets establish the core identity of your brand and ensure consistency across all other assets:

- Logo and Brand Mark: Primary and secondary logos, brand marks, and variations (e.g., black-and-white versions, icon versions).

- Brand Color Palette: A defined set of colors representing the brand across all platforms.

- Typography: Custom font choices and text styling guidelines.

- Brand Voice and Messaging: Documented tone, style, and key messaging guidelines.

- Brand Guidelines Document: A comprehensive guide outlining how all brand elements should be used to maintain consistency.

2. Product Development Assets

These assets support the creation of products and services that align with your brand's identity:

- Course Material Templates: Customizable templates for course slides, workbooks, and handouts.

- Video Assets: Intro/outro video templates, lower-thirds, and branded video overlays.

- E-Book/Guide Templates: Customizable layouts for digital books, guides, and reports.

- Custom Illustrations/Icons: Unique visual elements representing the brand's themes and values.

- Product Packaging Design: Digital mock-ups or physical designs for product packaging (if applicable).

- Brand Photography and Video Shoots: Professionally produced visual content aligning with the brand's identity.

3. Marketing and Sales Assets

These assets are used to attract, engage, and convert prospects into customers:

- Landing Pages: Fully branded landing pages for specific campaigns or product launches.

- Email Templates: Branded templates for email marketing campaigns, newsletters, and automated sequences.

- Digital Banners and Advertisements: High-quality ads for use on social media, Google Ads, and other digital platforms.

- Lead Magnets: Free downloadable content like PDFs, eBooks, checklists, or quizzes designed to capture leads.

- Social Media Content Templates: Consistent, on-brand templates for posts, stories, and social media ads.

- Custom Price Tags and Pricing Graphics: Visually appealing, branded pricing sheets and tags for products/services.

4. Client Engagement & Retention Assets

These assets are designed to engage existing clients and enhance their experience with your brand:

- Client Onboarding Kits: Welcome kits or guides that help new clients understand and navigate the brand's offerings.

- Branded Surveys and Feedback Forms: Tools for collecting client feedback in a manner consistent with the brand's voice.

- Loyalty Program Materials: Branded elements like loyalty cards, rewards program information, and digital badges.

- Customer Support Resources: FAQs, help documents, and how-to guides, all aligned with the brand's tone and style.

- Webinar and Event Templates: Branded slide decks, event banners, and virtual backgrounds for webinars and live events.

5. Advanced Personalization Assets

These assets are customized for specific audiences or highly tailored experiences:

- Personalized Product Recommendations: Systems or templates that allow for tailored product suggestions based on user behavior.

- Custom Interactive Content: Branded quizzes, calculators, or decision-making tools that engage users on a deeper level.

- Dynamic Email Content: Email campaigns that dynamically adjust content based on user data (e.g., purchase history, engagement level).

- Personalized Video Messages: Tailored video content for specific customers or customer segments, maintaining a strong personal touch.

6. In-House Systems & Automation Assets

These assets streamline and automate brand consistency across all platforms:

- Content Management Systems (CMS) Templates: Branded templates within the CMS for consistent content publishing.

- Workflow Automation Tools: Tools that automate repetitive tasks while ensuring all content adheres to brand guidelines.

- AI-Driven Content Creation Systems: Systems that automatically generate brand-consistent content using AI, such as blog posts, social media updates, and video scripts.

- Internal Training Modules: Branded training videos and materials for new hires or partners, ensuring they understand and maintain the brand's standards.

The Power of the Compounding Effect

When developing these brand assets, it's best to align your value propositions with your audience's six key demographic traits, as discussed in the audience definition process. Because our team at Simply Edit Pro meticulously handled the brand development and put together a comprehensive brand kit during the defining process, it took our development team just a few days to create all the necessary branded assets. Without a properly packaged and defined brand, this process could take months. This is a testament to the power of the compounding effect as you move through each step of brand and product development.

Understanding the MVP Concept

In the realm of product development, it's crucial to grasp the concept of an MVP, or Minimum Viable Product. While many may recognize the acronym as "Most Valuable Player" in sports, in business, it stands for the simplest version of a product that can be released to the market. The MVP includes only the core features necessary to solve the primary problems the product is intended to address, providing enough value to early adopters while allowing your development team to learn from actual usage.

According to a study by CB Insights, 42% of startups fail because they misjudge market needs. This statistic underscores the importance of an MVP—focusing on essential features from the beginning can prevent wasted resources on non-essential aspects that may not resonate with your target market. Additionally, an MVP allows for quicker iteration and feedback, helping you fine-tune your product and develop more comprehensive, tiered pricing structures down the road.

Educating Your Consumer

With a well-established MVP, you can now focus on developing ways to educate your consumer through webinars, workshops, and interactive content. One common mistake business owners make is assuming that consumers fully understand the value of their products and services. In reality, most consumers only grasp surface-level outcomes, which means the burden of comprehension is on you, the business owner.

A study by Edelman found that 63% of consumers need to hear company claims three to five times before they believe them. This highlights the need for consistent and clear communication. It's your job to demonstrate the full value and potential outcomes of your offerings. In Tavarus's case, we created a comprehensive webinar that provided an overview, educating new clients on how to navigate Dove Mastery's offerings and the outcomes they could expect.

Conclusion: The Strategic Path Forward

Product development is not just about creating assets; it's about strategically aligning those assets with your brand identity and audience needs. By categorizing assets into levels that correspond to different stages of the customer lifecycle, you can ensure consistency, relevance, and impact across all your brand's touchpoints.

Remember, the compounding effect of a well-defined brand accelerates every subsequent step in your business. By starting with a clear definition, developing an MVP, and educating your consumers, you set the stage for a successful product launch that resonates with your audience and drives growth.

CHAPTER 6

Distribution

Distribution Strategy Overview

I

n any successful project, distribution is key. It's not just about creating a great product; it's about ensuring that your product reaches the right audience through the right channels. In the case of the Dove Mastery project, our goal was to build a branded platform that could host a wide array of offerings—everything from courses and books to coaching services and speaking engagements. Below, you'll see an image representing the Dove Mastery website ecosystem, with tabs at the top reflecting this comprehensive suite of offerings.

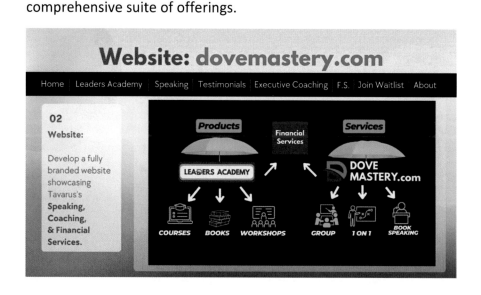

The Leaders Academy tab is a focal point of the website, hosting all Dove Mastery products such as courses, books, and workshops. On the right side under the services section, users can find options for group coaching, one-on-one coaching, and even a dedicated page to book Tavarus for speaking engagements.

This ecosystem is not just a website; it's a well-orchestrated distribution platform designed to guide users seamlessly through their journey with the Dove Mastery brand.

The Strategic Importance of Distribution

The ultimate goal for this distribution strategy was to create a centralized, branded platform that could effectively showcase and distribute Tavarus's offerings. However, this approach is just the beginning. As we move into the systemizing phase later in the book, we'll explore the benefits of a multichannel distribution strategy, which is crucial for maximizing reach and engagement.

A multichannel distribution strategy involves utilizing various platforms—such as social media, email, podcasts, and video platforms—to distribute your content and offerings. According to a report by Omnisend, marketers who used three or more channels in their campaigns saw a 287% higher purchase rate than those who only used a single channel. This underscores the importance of diversifying your distribution efforts to reach a broader audience.

For now, let's focus on the role of distribution within the product development phase of Dove Mastery. One of the most powerful concepts we implemented into the Dove Mastery website was the "Join Waitlist" tab. This feature was not just a marketing tool; it was a strategic move to build an engaged, pre-qualified audience for Tavarus's first group coaching sessions.

The Power of the Waitlist

Waitlists are a potent tool used by many successful companies and events to gauge market demand before a full launch. They serve as an early indicator of interest and can help you fine-tune your offerings based on real user data. In the case of Dove Mastery, the waitlist allows the opportunity to build a small trial audience that could participate in the initial group coaching meetings.

This approach aligns with a concept I learned from Daniel Priestley: marketing for signals of interest before launching your MVP (Minimum Viable Product). Especially for programs like group coaching, where getting a committed group of participants is crucial, a waitlist can provide valuable insights and a level of commitment from your potential clients.

Implementing the Scorecard-Waitlist Combo

To join the Dove Mastery waitlist, participants were required to complete a 15-question scorecard assessing their financial readiness. This scorecard was more than just a form; it was a dynamic tool designed to prequalify potential candidates for Dove Mastery's offerings, including the group coaching service. Once participants completed the scorecard, they were directed to a dynamic results/sales page where they could review their results and learn more about the services most relevant to them.

This scorecard-waitlist combination is a powerful tactic that you can implement in your next product rollout. It not only helps you gather signals of interest before going to market but also allows you to tailor your marketing efforts based on the insights gained from the scorecard responses.

According to a study by Harvard Business Review, companies that use data-driven marketing strategies are six times more likely to be profitable year-over-year. The scorecard approach fits perfectly within this strategy, as it provides valuable data on your audience before you've even launched your product. By understanding their readiness, needs, and interests, you can refine your offerings and marketing messages, increasing the likelihood of a successful launch.

Broadening Distribution Beyond the Website

As we expand our discussion into the systemizing phase, we'll explore how to broaden this distribution approach across multiple channels.

This includes leveraging social media, email marketing, podcasts, video platforms, and more to create a cohesive, omnipresent brand experience.

Multichannel distribution is not just a trend; it's a necessity in today's digital landscape. According to Salesforce's State of Marketing report, 76% of consumers prefer different channels depending on the context, which means meeting your audience where they are is more important than ever.

Conclusion: A Strategic Distribution Framework

The Dove Mastery project's distribution strategy serves as a framework that can be adapted and expanded for other brands. By starting with a centralized, branded platform and incorporating tools like waitlists and scorecards, you can create a robust distribution system that not only reaches your audience but also engages them at every stage of their journey.

Remember, distribution is not just about spreading your message; it's about creating meaningful connections with your audience through the channels they prefer. As we move forward in this book, we'll dive deeper into the strategies and systems that can help you build a multichannel distribution network that drives growth and success.

CHAPTER 7

Production Methods
for the Unavailable

AI Avatar Content Creation

M
any of us know the feeling of wishing we could be in two places at once. The reality of modern business, however, often demands it. On average, it takes 20-30 hours to create a high-quality YouTube video, including scripting, filming, editing, and post-production. Yet, 53% of business owners report that they can only dedicate 1-3 hours per week to content creation (Sources: Wyzowl, Buffer). This discrepancy is a significant contributor to the content deficit that plagues so many businesses today.

At Simply Edit Pro, we recognized this challenge and developed what we call "Production Methods for the Unavailable." With the rise of artificial intelligence, we set out to create standardized AI Avatar content systems that could revolutionize the way businesses produce content. Our approach involves utilizing cutting-edge AI Avatar software to create a digital copy of the key person of influence in your business. This digital avatar can then be used to generate content without the need for constant physical presence.

Once the AI Avatar is created, our award-winning editing team takes over. We develop content and digital products around your

AI Avatar, embellishing every piece through the lens of your brand identity kit. This ensures that all content maintains a high-quality, consistent look that resonates with your audience.

Our team specializes in building high-quality, monetized content, including:

- Training Videos

- Branded Social Media Content

- Monetized Courses

- YouTube Channel Development

- Branded Ad Campaigns

This technique has proven to be one of the most effective production methods not just for the unavailable, but period. Research has shown that video-based training improves information retention by 65%. Combine this with the fact that AI can reduce production costs by up to 50%, and you have a powerful, scalable, and affordable way to develop high volumes of content extraordinarily fast. We're talking about creating a decade's worth of content in just a few months.

The Turnkey Production Experience

To elevate our production methods even further, we added a 'white glove' element, creating a completely turnkey experience. Whether you need a training series, course, or book, our clients have the option to provide us with a simple overview of topics to cover, and our team handles the rest. We create the actual curriculum and dialogue, pairing this with our AI avatar methods to produce digital products in record time. The result is a plug-and-play experience that allows clients to launch fully developed content without lifting a finger.

Book Development with AI and Video

Let's delve into another innovative production method we developed for those who are unavailable: book development using AI and video. We faced a unique challenge when working with Tavarus Dove, who, despite his strengths as a speaker, coach, and financial expert, lacked the time necessary to write a full-length book. With Tavarus's hectic traveling schedule, he could only dedicate two days, with four hours each day, for filming and production.

Determined to innovate, my team crafted a radical book development system. This system involved creating a series of YouTube videos based on the sub-chapters of his book. We identified 8-10 chapters, each with 4 sub-chapters, resulting in a need for 30-40 videos, each ranging from 10-15 minutes, to thoroughly cover each concept.

Our challenge was to get all of the filming done in under two days. To do this, we developed a branded system that allowed Tavarus to efficiently execute each video topic. At the time, Tavarus was located across the country, so we shipped the necessary production gear and collaborated with his administration staff to operate the camera. Through Zoom sessions, we standardized camera settings and trained Tavarus and his team on the new branded format for efficiently executing videos.

Streamlined Video Production and Book Creation

First, we standardized the video introductions: "Welcome back to Dove Mastery, I'm your host Tavarus Dove, and today we're going to be covering [insert name of subchapter]." Then, we created a call to action (CTA) that would be recorded once and applied to the end of each video in the series. The CTA was designed to educate viewers about Dove Mastery's offerings and invite them to attend the webinar linked in the description. It also encouraged viewers to take the financial readiness scorecard we designed, generating interest for the group coaching waitlist.

With a well-defined introduction and CTA structure in place, the final step was to add the substance for each subchapter. Leveraging Tavarus's strengths as a speaker and financial expert, we prompted him with relevant questions adjacent to each subchapter of the book. Over the course of two Zoom sessions, my team successfully coached Tavarus through the entire 8-hour filming experience.

Turning Video Content into a Published Book

The results were astounding. Our diligent preparation and development systems provided Tavarus and his team with an efficient and comfortable experience, allowing us to create a 30-video series with over 5 hours of content. We then transcribed those five hours of video content and turned it into a 100+ page book.

To ensure the book was ready for publication, we performed multiple passes of editing, refining the dialogue and removing any direct or indirect references to the YouTube platform. This ensured that the text read as standalone book content.

The process created a "two birds, one stone" effect for Tavarus—within 8 hours, we essentially wrote an entire book and created a video series that could double as both an audiobook and monetizable videos for his YouTube channel. The content we produced was enough to post on YouTube once a week for almost an entire year.

The Power of High-Volume Content Systems

When it comes to creating high-volume content systems like this, having a specialized team with a well-defined brand is key. The snowball compounding effect it provides allows you to achieve incredible results, even when time is limited. This approach not only maximizes efficiency but also ensures that the content produced is of the highest quality, aligned with your brand's identity, and ready to engage your audience across multiple platforms.

This is a direct result of the innovative production methods we've developed at Simply Edit Pro, and it's one of my personal favorite strategies for those who are unavailable. By leveraging AI, video, and a well-coordinated team, we've created a scalable, efficient, and highly effective system for content creation that meets the demands of today's fast-paced business environment.

CHAPTER 8

Launch

Systemizing the Process

H

ow did we systemize all of this? We've discussed the three main elements of the development phase; now let's dive into how we built functional systems for Dove Mastery that can be replicated in other businesses. Below, you'll find a visual diagram illustrating the inner workings of this systemized approach.

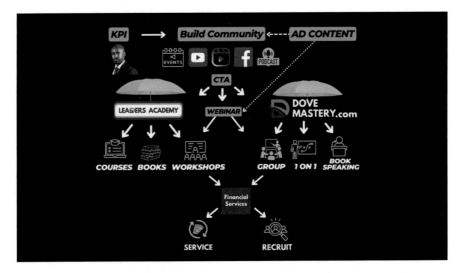

Starting from the top, we have the Key Person of Influence (KPI)—in this case, Tavarus. As the face of the Dove Mastery brand, Tavarus represents the brand publicly, speaking at events, appearing on podcasts, and uploading content to social media. The diagram highlights how a KPI like Tavarus plays a crucial role in distributing high volumes of content, such as the YouTube series we previously discussed. Over the next seven months, we'll be rolling out all 5 hours of YouTube videos, posting them consistently to keep the audience engaged.

Also included in the diagram is the annual social media ad content that we'll be running. Similar to the CTA designed for the YouTube-to-book series, this ad content invites viewers to attend a webinar where Tavarus literally walks them through a similar diagram, explaining how Dove Mastery works. It's a strategy I personally believe every business should incorporate into their annual ad content plan. As we've discussed, showing people how to use your company's offerings and the outcomes they create is crucial. Following this, we provide a specialized product or offer for those who attend the webinar, driving engagement and conversions.

The system is designed so that many potential customers will either attend the webinar or go directly to the most relevant product or service listed in the diagram. By the time prospects reach the end of their journey, they will either purchase a product or service, join the waitlist, or be fully educated on the company's offerings. Your business systems should have multiple checkpoints—opportunities to learn from your consumer or ethically capture their email to be remarketed to later.

This systemized approach, tailored specifically for the Dove Mastery brand, is modular and can be adapted for different sequences to attract consumers. While we found this approach to be highly effective for Dove Mastery, the elements within this diagram can serve as a template for systemizing other brands as well.

Building In-House Systems for Future Use

One of the final steps we took for Tavarus was creating in-house branded team assets, ensuring consistency and continuity across all future content. Typically, when working with high-end agencies, they will build in-house systems and branded assets for future production teams to utilize. We go a step further by creating actual training videos that showcase how different assets should be applied to specific formats of content. This ensures that, going forward, you always have a consistent look and feel that aligns with your custom brand kit.

Packaging all these elements together not only makes future production projects move ten times faster, especially when they've gone through the defining phase with us, but it also provides a lasting resource that your team can rely on. Whether you continue working with us or not, it's crucial to have these systems in place for yourself.

The Cost of Efficiency

Now, let's take a moment to address the cost of efficiency, particularly in relation to the Dove Mastery project. We understand that discussing production costs can sometimes feel a bit daunting, but our goal here is to be transparent and highlight the value that was delivered.

For the Dove Mastery project, the total cost of working with Simply Edit Pro was approximately $12,000. This might seem substantial at first glance, but when you consider the scope of what was accomplished—the development of a full video series, the creation of a 100+ page book, the design of branded digital assets, and the systemization of content distribution—the value becomes clear.

We're proud to offer our services on a subscription-based model, with affordable monthly payments starting at $2,000. This model allows our clients to get a lot done quickly, even if they're working on ambitious projects like writing a series of books, rapidly developing their social profiles, or creating a host of digital products like courses and workshops. It's designed to be scalable and accessible, providing high-quality results without the burden of a massive upfront cost.

To put this into perspective, if you were to piece together individual quotes from multiple vendors for the various elements we provided in the Dove Mastery project, the minimum market value would be roughly $92,000. That's a total savings of about $80,000—a significant figure that underscores the efficiency and value of our approach.

At Simply Edit Pro, we're committed to building, systemizing, and creating powerful, scalable, and affordable ways to develop high volumes of content on extraordinary timelines. By leveraging the power of high-volume content systems combined with AI tools, we're helping businesses like Dove Mastery overcome the content deficit and achieve their goals.

Conclusion: Investing in Your Brand's Future

Investing in a comprehensive content strategy is not just about the cost; it's about the long-term value and impact on your brand's success. The systems we built for Dove Mastery are a testament to what can be achieved with the right approach and the right team. We believe in providing our clients with exceptional value—saving them time, resources, and money—while delivering results that exceed expectations.

We love what we do, and we're passionate about helping businesses grow through innovative content solutions. Together, we can put an end to the content deficit and set your brand on a path to sustained success.

Visit **SimplyEditPro.com** for more information.

Struggling to Keep Up with Content Demands?

In today's fast-paced digital world, businesses must produce high-quality content consistently to stay competitive. But what happens when your content creation can't keep pace with your marketing goals? **The result is a content deficit—a** gap that can hold back your business from reaching its full potential.

The Content Deficit offers practical strategies and insights to help modern business owners close that gap and build a robust marketing pipeline. Whether you're an entrepreneur looking to grow your brand or a seasoned marketer aiming to streamline your efforts, this book will guide you through:

- Understanding The Content Deficit: **Learn what causes the gap and how it impacts your marketing.**
- Actionable Steps to Bridge the Gap: **Implement effective strategies to create a steady flow of content that drives results.**
- Leveraging Tools and AI Techniques: **Discover the best tools and techniques to enhance your content production and distribution.**

Unlock the Potential of Your Business by mastering the art of content creation and filling the void that's holding you back.

About the Author:
Dallen Taylor, Founder of Simply Edit Pro, is a dynamic digital marketing expert, and content strategist. At just 28, Dallen has already transformed the way businesses approach their content challenges, leveraging innovative strategies to drive real results. With a track record of empowering business owners to achieve their marketing goals, **Dallen's practical insights have been the catalyst for countless brands to thrive in today's competitive landscape.**

Made in the USA
Las Vegas, NV
12 September 2024

95205582R00029